More ILLUSTRATED
WRINKLIES'
WIT & WISDOM

First published in Great Britain in 2009 by Prion
an imprint of the Carlton Publishing Group
20 Mortimer Street
London W1T 3JW

10 9 8 7 6 5 4 3 2 1

A catalogue record for this book is available from the British Library
The quotations in this book originally appeared in *Wrinklies' Wit & Wisdom Rides Again*

ISBN 978-1-85375-691-7

Printed in Dubai

More ILLUSTRATED
WRINKLIES'
WIT & WISDOM

Humorous Quotes
About Getting On a Bit

Compiled by Alison Rattle & Allison Vale

PRION

Contents

Introduction

Growing old is not what it used to be. Thanks to huge advances in medical science and the propensity of the media to bombard us with sleek visions of ageless, airbrushed celebrities, breaking down the age barrier is easier than ever. Who now thinks of 50 or even 60 as being particularly old? Mick Jagger with his pants pulled over his belly; Joan Collins in wrinkled support tights? Not likely! Our healthier lifestyles and the invention of lycra undergarments have driven the physical signs of ageing back at least a decade. Look around any pub, theatre or nightclub, and you'll be sure to see plenty of vintage verve. The silver set are out there grabbing life by the throat as much, if not more so, than the younger generation.

Life for the over 50s has never been better. Women can now expect to live well into their 80s with men following close on their heels. This has given birth to an anti-ageing fad which takes full advantage of this spectacular longevity. The crossover from adulthood into old age is becoming progressively blurred. With the growing popularity and acceptability of cosmetic surgery, many people now choose to deny the ageing process altogether (some with more success than others – not mentioning any names.)

We must not forget however, that the autumn years serve their own purpose and should be embraced. There is an African proverb that illustrates beautifully how other cultures elevate age: "The death of an old person is like the loss of a library."

Western societies are losing sight of this like never before. From both sides of the Atlantic we risk being overwhelmed by the new cult of celebrity. It is an inexhaustible quarry: periodically, someone sees fit to carve out another vacuous wannabe, bursting with youth, sex appeal and a psychotic need for fame. Often, talent is an irrelevance. Anyone willing to play strip poker live on national TV, eat unimaginable grubs in an Australian jungle, or disgrace themselves on a TV talent show, can grab their fleeting 15 minutes. It's so dreary.

This compilation challenges the stereotypes that this cult of celebrity would have us adopt. It celebrates the geniuses and giants of our time. The kind of professional entertainers who can still pull together three generations of a family around the TV and guarantee that everyone's laughing. The heavyweight actors who have put in decades of graft and now lend an emotional depth and gravitas to any scene.

The names in this collection have energy, vibrancy and longevity. Retirement, for many of them, is out of the question. They are sexy, sassy and sophisticated seniors who are still smouldering on screen and can give any skimpily clad "artiste" something to wail about. Laugh along with Woody Allen, John Cleese, Julie Walters, Whoopi Goldberg and more, as they observe life's joys, trials and irritations.

The wrinkly years are not to be denied, reviled or feared, but to be welcomed and enjoyed. Forget a quiet, dignified old age and party on!

Alison Rattle & Allison Vale

Growing Old is...

…when "getting lucky" means finding your car in the car park.

…when an "all nighter" means not getting up to pee.

…when "getting a little action" means you don't need to eat any fibre.

…when you're told to slow down by the doctor instead of the police.

…when going bra-less pulls all the wrinkles out of your face.

…when your wife says, "Let's go upstairs and make love," and you answer, "Honey, I can't do both!"

…when you remember when it cost more to run a car than to park it.

Youthful Thinking

Youth would be an ideal state if it came a little later in life.

Herbert Asquith

Youth is a wonderful thing. What a crime to waste it on children.

George Bernard Shaw

It is better to waste one's youth than to do nothing with it at all.

Georges Courteline

I'm aiming by the time I'm 50 to stop being an adolescent.

Wendy Cope

Youth is like spring, an over praised season.

Samuel Butler

Old age at least gives me an excuse for not being very good at things that I was not very good at when I was young.

Thomas Sowell

We are only young once. That is all society can stand.

Bob Bowen

Till Death Us Do Part

My wife and I were happy for 20 years. Then we met.

Rodney Dangerfield

I married the first man I ever kissed. When I tell this to my children they just about throw up.

Barbara Bush

We take time to go to a restaurant two times a week. A little candlelight, dinner, soft music and dancing. She goes Tuesdays, I go Fridays.

Henny Youngman

My wife and I tried to breakfast together, but we had to stop or our marriage would have been wrecked.

Winston Churchill

When asked his secret of love, being married 54 years to the same person, he said, 'Ruth and I are happily incompatible.'

Billy Graham

I haven't spoken to my wife in years. I didn't want to interrupt her.

Rodney Dangerfield

No man or woman really knows what perfect love is until they have been married a quarter of a century.

Mark Twain

My new wife is 32 and I'm 70. She's rejuvenated me totally. It's so exciting to see life through the eyes of a modern girl.

Wilbur Smith

There is no greater happiness for a man than approaching a door at the end of a day knowing someone on the other side of that door is waiting for the sound of his footsteps.

Ronald Reagan

The other night I said to my wife Ruth, 'Do you feel that the sex and excitement have gone out of our marriage?' She said, 'I'll discuss it with you during the next commercial.'

Milton Berle

One Christmas my husband gave me a chenille hand-knitted bobble hat. It was like we'd never met. I opened it and I said, 'Did you not like me when you bought me this?'

Arabella Weir

We were just happy to be in the same room together.

Judi Dench, *on her long marriage to Michael Williams.*

The man or woman you really love will never grow old to you. Through the wrinkles of time, through the bowed frame of years, you will always see the dear face and feel the warm heart union of your eternal love.

Alfred A. Montapert

My wife Mary and I have been married for 47 years and not once have we had an argument serious enough to consider divorce; murder, yes, but divorce, never.

Jack Benny

After about 20 years of marriage, I'm finally starting to scratch the surface of that one. And I think the answer lies somewhere between conversation and chocolate.

Mel Gibson, when asked if he knew what women want.

I was married for 30 years. Isn't that enough? I've had my share of dirty underwear on the floor.

Martha Stewart

Your marriage is in trouble if your wife says, "You're only interested in one thing," and you can't remember what it is.

Milton Berle

Sexy at Sixty

I know nothing about sex because I was always married.

Zsa Zsa Gabor

Before we make love my husband takes a painkiller.

Joan Rivers

The Three Ages of Marriage: 20 is when you watch the TV after. 40 is when you watch the TV during. 60 is when you watch the TV instead.

Anon

After a man passes 60, his mischief is mainly in his head.

Washington Irving

What is a younger woman? I'm pretty old, so almost every woman is younger than me.

Jack Nicholson

It seems that after the age of 50, I began to age at the rate of about three years per year. I began falling asleep 15 minutes into an episode of *Seinfeld*. I also began falling asleep during sex rather than after.

Anon

As you get older, you don't get as horny – I don't take as many cold showers a day as I used to.

Tom Jones

The pleasures that once were heaven, look silly at 67.

Noel Coward

If you can't have fun as an ageing sex symbol when you hit 60, I don't know what will become of you.

Raquel Welch

My love life is terrible. The last time I was inside a woman was when I visited the Statue of Liberty.

Woody Allen

I have so little sex appeal that my gynaecologist calls me "sir".

Joan Rivers

In my outrageous 20s, I asked a charming, chatty Englishwoman I'd met in Villefranche when people stopped having sex. "It's no good asking me, my dear," she said. "I'm only 83."

Anon

I base my fashion taste on what doesn't itch.

Gilda Radner

Viva Viagra

I only take Viagra when I am with more than one woman.

Jack Nicholson

At my age, I'm envious of a stiff wind.

Rodney Dangerfield

Everything that goes up must come down. But there comes a time when not everything that's down can come up.

George Burns

An elderly gentleman went to the local drugstore and asked the pharmacist for Viagra. The pharmacist said, "That's no problem. How many do you want?" The man replied, "Just a few, maybe half a dozen, but can you cut each one into four pieces?" The pharmacist said, "That's too small a dose. That won't get you through sex." The gentleman said, "Oh, that's all right. I'm past 80 years old, and I don't even think about sex any more. I just want it to stick out far enough so I don't pee on my shoes."

Anon

If I marry again at my age, I'll go on honeymoon to Viagra Falls.

George Burns

Sagacity
WISDOM

And in the end, it's not the years in your life that count. It's the life in your years.

Abraham Lincoln

All would live long, but none would be old.

Benjamin Franklin

The older I grow, the more I listen to people who don't say much.

Germain G. Glidden

The man who views the world at 50 the same as he did at 20 has wasted 30 years of his life.

Muhammad Ali

If you wait, all that happens is that you get older.

Mario Andretti

I shall not waste my days trying to prolong them.

Ian L. Fleming

The thing you realize as you get older is that parents don't know what the hell they're doing and neither will you when you get to be a parent.

Mark Hoppus

You can tell a lot about a fellow's character by his way of eating jellybeans.

Ronald Reagan

Wisdom doesn't necessarily come with age. Sometimes age just shows up all by itself.

Tom Wilson

Perhaps one has to be very old before one learns to be amused rather than shocked.

Pearl S. Buck

To be 70 years young is sometimes far more cheerful and hopeful than to be 40 years old.

Oliver Wendell Holmes Jr.

You don't stop laughing when you grow old; you grow old when you stop laughing.

Anon

Women on Ageing

I have to be careful to get out before I become the grotesque caricature of a hatchet-faced woman with big knockers.

Jamie Lee Curtis

I shall not grow conservative with age.

Elizabeth Cady Stanton

A woman my age is not supposed to be attractive or sexually appealing. I just get kinda tired of that.

Kathleen Turner

When I passed 40 I dropped pretence, 'cause men like women who got some sense.

Maya Angelou

I do resent that when you're in the most cool, powerful time of your life, which is your 40s, you're put out to pasture. I think women are so much cooler when they're older. So it's a drag that we're not allowed to age.

Rosanna Arquette

I am really looking forward as I get older and older, to being less and less nice.

Annette Bening

I spend most of my time puffing up my ego… till I'm this big ego thing… but it doesn't take much for it to be pricked, and then I'm just this deflated, shrivelled, shamed old woman with a bit of wee running down my legs.

Jenny Eclair, Grumpy Old Women.

You end up as you deserve. In old age you must put up with the face, the friends, the health, and the children you have earned.

Fay Weldon

Every woman over 50 should stay in bed until noon.

Mamie Eisenhower

I've had to tone it down a bit. But I've still got fabulous legs and wear mini-skirts. I'll keep wearing bikinis till I'm 80… I will grow old gracefully in public – and disgracefully in private.

Jerry Hall

If you obey all the rules, you miss all the fun.

Katharine Hepburn

Men on Ageing

When our memories outweigh our dreams, we have grown old.

Bill Clinton

Men become old, but they never become good.

Oscar Wilde

As men get older, their toys get more expensive.

Marvin Davis

I think a lot about getting old. I don't want to be one of those 70-year-olds who still want lots of sex.

Rupert Everett

I think when the full horror of being 50 hits you; you should stay home and have a good cry.

Alan Bleasdale

At my age, I want to wake up and see sunshine pouring in through the windows every day.

John Cleese

Some mornings, it's just not worth chewing through the leather straps.

Emo Philips

I still find each day too short for all the thoughts I want to think, all the walks I want to take, all the books I want to read, and all the friends I want to see.

John Burroughs

Most men do not mature, they simply grow taller.

Leo Rosten

A man can be much amused when he hears himself seriously called an old man for the first time.

T. Kinnes

Old age: I fall asleep during the funerals of my friends.

Mason Cooley

I'm only two years older than Brad Pitt, but I look a lot older, which used to greatly frustrate me. It doesn't any more.

George Clooney

Listen to Your Elders

Look to the future, because that is where you'll spend the rest of your life.

George Burns

Don't take life too seriously; you'll never get out of it alive.

Elbert Hubbard

Don't smoke too much, drink too much, eat too much or work too much. We're all on the road to the grave – but there's no need to be in the passing lane.

Robert Orben

There are times not to flirt. When you're sick. When you're with children. When you're on the witness stand.

Joyce Jillson

Always read stuff that will make you look good if you die in the middle of it.

P.J. O'Rourke

Never kick a fresh turd on a hot day.

Harry S. Truman

Go through your phone book, call people and ask them to drive you to the airport. The ones who will drive you are your true friends. The rest aren't bad people; they're just acquaintances.

Jay Leno

You can't have everything. Where would you put it?

Steven Wright

In real life, I assure you, there is no such thing as algebra.

Fran Lebowitz

Whatever you want to do, do it now. There are only so many tomorrows.

Michael Landon

You can add years to your life by wearing your pants backwards.

Johnny Carson

34

Golden Oldies

FAMOUS OLDIES

When you're a young man, Macbeth is a character part. When you're older, it's a straight part.

Laurence Olivier

Old age is like everything else. To make a success of it, you've got to start young.

Fred Astaire

I have the body of an 18-year-old. I keep it in the fridge.

Spike Milligan

One of the advantages of ageing is losing obsession about work and being able to spend some more time with your family.

Clint Eastwood

In his later years Pablo Picasso was not allowed to roam an art gallery unattended, for he had previously been discovered in the act of trying to improve on one of his old masterpieces.

Anon

I feel like an old geezer!… Well, I am an old geezer.

Terry Wogan

I am affectionately known by Elton John as either Sylvia Disc or the Bionic Christian.

Sir Cliff Richard

In two years time I will be 50. But age doesn't hold any terrors for me because I feel stronger than ever.

Pierce Brosnan

Getting old is a fascinating thing. The older you get, the older you want to get.

Keith Richards

I will actually say, "Look, I'm very old and I'm very bored with you all, and I'm leaving." It's one of the advantages of ageing – you can be eccentric and rude.

Sheila Hancock, Grumpy Old Women.

It is far better to be out with beautiful girls than be an old fart in the pub talking about what you were like in the 60s.

Mick Jagger

Golfing Grandpas

Golf is a good walk spoiled.

Mark Twain

Golf is more fun than walking naked in a strange place, but not much.

Buddy Hackett

Playing golf is like going to a strip joint. After 18 holes you're tired and most of your balls are missing.

Tim Allen

The uglier a man's legs are, the better he plays golf – it's almost a law.

H.G. Wells

Golf is a fascinating game. It has taken me nearly 40 years to discover that I can't play it.

Ted Ray

Sex and golf are the two things you can enjoy even if you're not good at them.

Kevin Costner

I know I'm getting better at golf because I'm hitting fewer spectators.

Gerald Ford

If you think it's hard to meet new people, try picking up the wrong golf ball.

Jack Lemmon

Golf is a day spent in a round of strenuous idleness.

William Wordsworth

It is almost impossible to remember how tragic a place the world is when one is playing golf.

Robert Lynd

Golf: a game where white men can dress up as black pimps and get away with it.

Robin Williams

Geriatric Gardening

To get the best results you must talk to your vegetables.

Prince Charles

I want Death to find me planting my cabbages.

Michel De Montaigne

If you want to be happy for a short time, get drunk; happy for a long time, fall in love; happy forever, take up gardening.

Arthur Smith

Then again, if the plant is slow growing, and you are getting older, you may want to start with a larger plant. I find myself buying larger plants each year.

Bill Cannon

Old gardeners never die. They just spade away and then throw in the trowel.

Herbert V. Prochnow

Cherry trees will blossom every year, but I'll disappear for good, one of these days.

Philip Whalen

Spicing up the Twilight Years

Once the travel bug bites there is no known antidote, and I know
that I shall be happily infected until the end of my life.

Michael Palin

Football and cookery are the two most important subjects in this
country.

Delia Smith

Life may not be the party we hoped for, but while we are here we
might as well dance.

J. Williams

Give a man a fish and he has food for a day. Teach him how to
fish and you can get rid of him for the entire weekend.

Zenna Schaffer

There is a very fine line between "hobby" and "mental illness".

Dave Barry

I usually take a two-hour nap from one to four.

Yogi Berra

Hell, if I'd jumped on all the dames I'm supposed to have jumped on, I'd have had no time to go fishing.

Clark Gable

Fishing is boring, unless you catch an actual fish, and then it is disgusting.

Dave Barry

There's a fine line between fishing and just standing on the shore like an idiot.

Steven Wright

Skiing combines outdoor fun with knocking down trees with your face.

Dave Barry

The difference between sex and death is that with death you can do it alone and no one is going to make fun of you.

Woody Allen

I have a rare intolerance which means I can only drink fermented liquids such as gin.

Julie Walters

I'm Gonna Live Forever

The secret of longevity is to keep breathing.

Sophie Tucker

If man were immortal, do you realize what his meat bills would be?

Woody Allen

To lengthen thy life, lessen thy meals.

Benjamin Franklin

The secret to a long life is to stay busy, get plenty of exercise, and don't drink too much. Then again, don't drink too little.

Hermann Smith-Johansson, at age 103.

Pretend to be dumb, that's the only way to reach old age.

Friedrich Dürrenmatt

A 90-year-old man was asked to what he attributed his longevity. "I reckon", he said, with a twinkle in his eye, "it's because most nights I went to bed and slept when I should have sat up and worried."

Dorothea Kent

If you live to the age of 100 you've made it because very few people die past the age of 100.

George Burns

My formula for living is quite simple. I get up in the morning and I go to bed at night. In between, I occupy myself as best I can.

Cary Grant

The only real way to look younger is not to be born so soon.

Charles M. Schulz

I wanna live 'til I die, no more, no less.

Eddie Izzard

Ageing seems to be the only available way to live a long life.

Daniel Auber

We could certainly slow the ageing process down if it had to work its way through Congress.

Anon

There's one advantage to being 102. No peer pressure.

Dennis Wolfberg

My secret for staying young is good food, plenty of rest, and a make-up man with a spray gun.

Bob Hope

I'd like to grow very old as slowly as possible.

Irene Mayer Selznick

My only fear is that I may live too long. This would be a subject of dread to me.

Thomas Jefferson

I would not live forever, because we should not live forever, because if we were supposed to live forever, then we would live forever, but we cannot live forever, which is why I would not live forever.

Miss Alabama, 1994 Miss USA contest.

He had decided to live forever or die in the attempt.

Joseph Heller

Money is something you make in case you don't die.

Max Asnas

Many Happy Returns

Most of us can remember a time when a birthday, especially if it was one's own, brightened the world as if a second sun had risen.

Robert Lynd

It is lovely, when I forget all birthdays, including my own, to find that somebody remembers me.

Ellen Glasgow

I always add a year to myself, so I'm prepared for my next birthday. So when I was 39, I was already 40.

Nicolas Cage

When I was a kid I could toast marshmallows over my birthday candles. Now I could roast a turkey!

Anon

You still chase women, but only downhill.

Bob Hope, on turning 70.

There comes a time when you should stop expecting other people to make a big deal about your birthday. That time is age 11.

Dave Barry

When a man has a birthday, he takes a day off. When a woman has a birthday, she takes at least three years off.

Joan Rivers

The best birthdays of all are those that haven't arrived yet.

Robert Orben

From our birthday, until we die, is but the winking of an eye.

William Butler Yeats

Last year my birthday cake looked like a prairie fire.

Rodney Dangerfield

You are never too old to set another goal or to dream a new dream.

Les Brown

You Can Teach an Old Dog New Tricks

When I was young I was amazed at Plutarch's statement that the elder Cato began at the age of 80 to learn Greek. I am amazed no longer. Old age is ready to undertake tasks that youth shirked because they would take too long.

W. Somerset Maugham

I enjoy going to the centre because I always get a lovely smile from the ladies there and I can impress them with new computer tips.

Lady, *100, attending computer classes.*

You are never too old. One of many examples, Grandma Moses (1860–1961), she started painting in her late 70s. She is best known for her documentary paintings of rural life. If you ever think you are too old, think of Grandma Moses!

Catherine Pulsifer

I'm having difficulty getting the doctors around here to sign the appropriate form.

Spike Milligan, *on seeking permission to celebrate his 80th birthday with a 12,000 foot skydive.*

Retirement is a Dirty Word

Retirement at 65 is ridiculous. When I was 65 I still had pimples.

George Burns

Never retire. Michelangelo was carving the *Rondanini* just before he died at 89. Verdi finished his opera *Falstaff* at 80. And the 80-year-old artist Goya scrawled on a drawing, "I am still learning".

Dr. W. Gifford-Jones

On announcing his retirement: You can only milk a cow for so long, then you're left holding the pail.

Hank Aaron

I'm mad, you know? I don't think of retiring at all.

Paul McCartney

People are always asking me when I'm going to retire. Why should I? I'm still making movies, and I'm a senior citizen, so I can see myself at half price.

George Burns

When old, retire from work, but not from life.

M.K. Soni

At 85 you can only think ahead for the next 50 years or so.

Chuck Jones, on signing a long-term contract with Warner Brothers.

Don't retire, retread!

Robert Otterbourg

When a man retires and time is no longer a matter of urgent importance, his colleagues generally present him with a watch.

R.C. Sherriff

Retirement: That's when you return from work one day and say, "Hi, honey, I'm home – forever."

Gene Perret

Retirement? You're talking about death, right?

Robert Altman

Retirement kills more people than hard work ever did.

Malcolm Forbes

The trouble with retirement is that you never get a day off.

Abe Lemons

Retirement: It's nice to get out of the rat race, but you have to learn to get along with less cheese.

Gene Perret

I love working. It's what I do best, and if I didn't work and tried to slow down, I'd just become a boring old fart.

Rik Mayall

Retirement is wonderful. It's doing nothing without worrying about getting caught at it.

Gene Perret

The question isn't at what age I want to retire, it's at what income.

George Foreman

Once it was impossible to find any Bond villains older than myself, I retired.

Roger Moore

Retirement must be wonderful. I mean, you can suck in your stomach for only so long.

Burt Reynolds

Retirement - now life begins.

Catherine Pulsifer

Crowning Glory

By common consent, grey hairs are a crown of glory: the only object of respect that can never excite envy.

George Bancroft

There is only one cure for grey hair. It was invented by a Frenchman. It is called the guillotine.

P.G. Wodehouse

It is not by the grey of the hair that one knows the age of the heart.

Edward Bulwer-Lytton

It seems no more than right that men should seize time by the forelock, for the rude old fellow, sooner or later, pulls all their hair out.

George Dennison Prentice

There is more felicity on the far side of baldness than young men can possibly imagine.

Logan Pearsall Smith

Grey hair is God's graffiti.

Bill Cosby

I'm entering the "metallic years"; silver in my hair, gold in my teeth and lead in my bottom!

Anon

On the bright side of life you will probably save a lot on shampoo when getting old and bald, and no longer have to suffer from thwarted and long gone ambitions.

T. Kinnes

My husband was bending over to tie my three-year-old's shoes. That's when I noticed my son Ben staring at my husband's head. He gently touched the slightly thinning spot of hair and said in a concerned voice, "Daddy, you have a hole in your head. Does it hurt?" After a pause, I heard my husband's murmured reply, "Not physically."

Reader's Digest

I'm not really bald. I just have a very wide parting.

Anon

The simple truth is that balding African-American men look cool when they shave their heads, whereas balding white men look like giant thumbs.

Dave Barry

We're all born bald, baby.

Telly Savalas

I'm not bald… I'm just taller than my hair.

Clive Anderson

The secret of my success is my hairspray.

Richard Gere

A man is usually bald four or five years before he knows it.

Ed Howe

The worst thing a man can do is go bald. Never let yourself go bald.

Donald Trump

He's the kind of guy that when he dies, he's going up to heaven and give God a bad time for making him bald.

Marlon Brando, on Frank Sinatra.

It's a question that I find like asking somebody, 'Did you have a breast implant?' or 'When did you get your lobotomy?

William Shatner, when asked if he wore a hairpiece.

My hairdresser actually spends more time digging hair out of my ears than off the top or back of my head.

Des Lynam, Grumpy Old Men.

Teething Troubles

I had very good dentures once. Some magnificent gold work. It's the only form of jewellery a man can wear that women fully appreciate.

Graham Greene

Dentures: Two rows of artificial ivories that may be removed periodically to frighten one's grandchildren or provide accompaniment to Spanish music.

Anon

It is after you have lost your teeth that you can afford to buy steaks.

Pierre Auguste Renoir

We idolized the Beatles, except for those of us who idolized the Rolling Stones, who in those days still had many of their original teeth.

Dave Barry

I don't have false teeth. Do you think I'd buy teeth like these?

Carol Burnett

Every tooth in a man's head is more valuable than a diamond.

Miguel de Cervantes

I Shall Wear Purple

After 50 a man discovers he does not need more than one suit.

Clifton Fadiman

Being home on a Friday night with the old man, an Indian take-away and a nice bottle of wine, and there's something on the telly, oh, I like that. I'm in my dressing gown, I mean it's not a weird dressing gown, it's not one of those quilted old lady ones. It's Cath Kidston. It's quite a funky dressing gown… don't get me wrong. I'm not that old.

Jenny Eclair, Grumpy Old Women.

If women dressed for men, the stores wouldn't sell much – just an occasional sun visor.

Groucho Marx

Underwear makes me uncomfortable and besides my parts have to breathe.

Jean Harlow

Trying on pants is one of the most humiliating things a man can suffer that doesn't involve a woman.

Larry David

You'd be surprised how much it costs to look this cheap.

Dolly Parton

I am 56 years old, an age when many women tend not to be noticed as we plod about in our extra wide, midi–heeled sensible shoes.

Sue Townsend

You can say what you like about long dresses, but they cover a multitude of shins.

Mae West

She looked as if she had been poured into her clothes and had forgotten to say "when".

P. G. Wodehouse

Brevity is the soul of lingerie.

Dorothy Parker

Dress simply. If you wear a dinner jacket, don't wear anything else on it… like lunch or dinner.

George Burns

Nothing goes out of fashion sooner than a long dress with a very low neck.

Coco Chanel

The only man I know who behaves sensibly is my tailor; he takes my measurements anew each time he sees me. The rest go on with their old measurements and expect me to fit them.

George Bernard Shaw

If God had meant us to walk around naked, he would never have invented the wicker chair.

Erma Bombeck

How on earth did Gandhi manage to walk so far in flip-flops? I can't last ten minutes in mine.

Mrs. Merton

I don't think I would've worn thongs even when I was young and trying very hard. No, that's ridiculous. You might as well go without knickers at all.

Annette Crosbie, Grumpy Old Women.

Women's clothes: never wear anything that panics the cat.

P.J. O'Rourke

I know what Victoria's Secret is. The secret is that nobody older than 30 can fit into their stuff.

Sima Jacobson

Young at Heart

He says he feels young at heart but slightly older in other places.

Anon

Another belief of mine: that everyone else my age is an adult, whereas I am merely in disguise.

Margaret Atwood

You can't help getting older, but you don't have to get old.

George Burns

You're only young once, but you can be immature forever.

John Greier

One starts to get young at the age of 60 and then it is too late.

Pablo Picasso

My veins are filled once a week with a Neapolitan carpet cleaner distilled from the Adriatic and I am as bald as an egg. However, I still get around and am mean to cats.

John Cheever

Setting a good example for your children takes all the fun out of middle age.

William Feather

I have spent my whole life – up to a minute ago – being younger than I am now.

John Ciardi

Except for an occasional heart attack I feel as young as I ever did.

Robert Benchley

Try to keep your soul young and quivering right up to old age.

George Sand

Life would be infinitely happier if we could only be born at the age of 80 and gradually approach 18.

Mark Twain

Now that I'm old [clothes shopping] has become entirely frustrating because there is nothing for me to wear in the shops. Nothing. I mean, I'm not going to wear hipster pants, am I? If I wear hipster pants and I sit down, I'll shoot out the back of them. It's not on.

Germaine Greer, Grumpy Old Women.

Over the Hill

I'm so old they've cancelled my blood type.

Bob Hope

I'd rather be over the hill than under it.

Anon

To live beyond 80 is an exaggeration, almost an excess.

Antonio Callado

Just remember, once you're over the hill you begin to pick up speed.

Charles M. Schulz

You know you're over the hill when the only whistles you get are from the tea kettle.

Anon

I didn't get old on purpose, it just happened. If you're lucky it could happen to you.

Andy Rooney

I'm too beat-up and old now to be a sex symbol.

Mel Gibson

I'd Rather Have a Cup of Tea

Growing old is when you resent the swimsuit issue of *Sports Illustrated* because there are fewer articles to read.

George Burns

Everyone probably thinks that I'm a raving nymphomaniac, that I have an insatiable sexual appetite, when the truth is I'd rather read a book.

Madonna

Middle age is having a choice of two temptations and choosing the one that will get you home earlier.

Dan Bennett

Now that I think of it, I wish I had been a hellraiser when I was 30 years old. I tried it when I was 50 but I always got sleepy.

Groucho Marx

I don't want to snog old men, with their yellow horrible teeth, old crinkly skin and hairy moles.

Cilla Black

Thank God! Now I realize I've been chained to an idiot for the last 60 years of my life!

Kingsley Amis at 70, on his lost libido.

I haven't had sex in eight months. To be honest, I now prefer to go bowling.

Anon

As I get older, I just prefer to knit.

Tracey Ullman

I'm at the age where I want two girls. In case I fall asleep they will have someone to talk to.

Rodney Dangerfield

Sex is a bad thing because it rumples the clothes.

Jackie Onassis

I am happy now that Charles calls on my bedchamber less frequently than of old. As it is, I now endure but two calls a week and when I hear his steps outside my door I lie down on my bed, close my eyes, open my legs and think of England.

Lady Alice Hillingdon

The Pipe and Slipper Brigade
SMOKING

Apparently cigarettes contain embalming fluid. This explains why I'm possibly the best-preserved woman in Britain.

Sue Carroll

I used to smoke all the time but four years ago I changed my smoking habit to smoke only when I'm drinking. However, this policy has had an adverse effect on my drinking habits.

Tommy Walsh

I might smoke more.

Jeremy Irons, *announcing his New Year resolution.*

I enjoy it too much.

David Bowie, *explaining why he will never give up smoking.*

Oh, I like smoking, I do. I smoke for my health, my mental health. Tobacco gives you little pauses, a rest from life. I don't suppose anyone smoking a pipe would have road rage, would they?

David Hockney

If I'm seen smoking in the street, people should come up to me and say thank you very much for keeping my tax bill down.

Jeremy Clarkson

If I cannot smoke in heaven, then I shall not go.

Mark Twain

I finally quit smoking by using the patch. I put six of them over my mouth.

Wendy Liebman

Giving up smoking is the easiest thing in the world. I know because I've done it thousands of times.

Mark Twain

They say if you smoke you knock off ten years. But it's the last ten. What do you miss? The drooling years?

John Mendoza

I've been smoking for 30 years now and there's nothing wrong with my lung.

Freddie Starr

Beer, it's the best damn drink in the world.

Jack Nicholson

Pass the Port

DRINK

I have been advised by the best medical authority, at my age, not to attempt to give up alcohol.

W.C. Fields

A man is a fool if he drinks before he reaches the age of 50, and a fool if he doesn't afterward.

Frank Lloyd Wright

I exercise strong self-control. I never drink anything stronger than gin before breakfast.

W.C. Fields

You're not drunk if you can lie on the floor without holding on.

Joe E. Lewis

Beer is proof that God loves us and wants us to be happy.

Benjamin Franklin

One more drink and I'll be under the host.

Dorothy Parker

I'm not a heavy drinker; I can sometimes go for hours without touching a drop.

Noel Coward

I feel sorry for people who don't drink. They wake up in the morning and that's the best they're going to feel all day.

Dean Martin

A woman drove me to drink and I didn't even have the decency to thank her.

W.C. Fields

Milk is for babies. When you grow up you have to drink beer.

Arnold Schwarzenegger

I drink too much. The last time I gave a urine sample it had an olive in it.

Rodney Dangerfield

When I was a practising alcoholic, I was unbelievable. One side effect was immense suspicion: I'd come off tour like Inspector Clouseau on acid. 'Where's this cornflake come from? It wasn't here before.'

Ozzy Osbourne

Fading Away
MEMORY LOSS

As you get older three things happen. The first is your memory goes, and I can't remember the other two.

Sir Norman Wisdom

Just sometimes you bump into people and you think, 'You're my best friend, aren't you? I recognize you. Ooh, you're looking old. What's your name?'

Jenny Eclair, Grumpy Old Women.

Did you ever walk in a room and forget why you walked in? I think that's how dogs spend their lives.

Sue Murphy

My memory is going. I brush my teeth, and then ten minutes later I go back and have to feel the toothbrush. Is it wet? Did I just brush them?

Terry Gilliam

Senior Moments

For those of you haven't read the book, it's being published tomorrow.

David Frost

And there's the Victoria Memorial, built as a memorial to Victoria.

David Dimbleby

The Holocaust was an obscene period in our nation's history…
this century's history… We all lived in this century. I didn't live in
this century.

Dan Quayle

Was it you or your brother who was killed in the war?

Rev. William Spooner

Republicans understand the importance of bondage between a
mother and child.

Dan Quayle

I haven't read any of the autobiographies about me.

Elizabeth Taylor

I've always thought that under populated countries in Africa are vastly under polluted.

Lawrence Summers, *chief economist of the World Bank.*

He hits from both sides of the plate. He's amphibious.

Yogi Berra

One year ago today, the time for excuse-making has come to an end.

George W. Bush

Outside of the killings, Washington has one of the lowest crime rates in the country.

Mayor Marion Barry, *Washington, D.C.*

And so, in my State of the – my State of the Union – or state – my speech to the nation, whatever you want to call it, speech to the nation – I asked Americans to give 4,000 years – 4,000 hours over the next – the rest of your life – of service to America. That's what I asked – 4,000 hours.

George W. Bush

The nice thing about being senile is you can hide your own Easter eggs.

Anon

Driving Miss Daisy

I suppose when I am driving, particularly in London, the thing that makes me angriest is cyclists, the anarchists of the road… they weave in and out, ignore the traffic lights and then if you dare go anywhere near them, they scream at you like banshees. There's this extraordinary assumption that we will all have to get out of their way. But they can do what they damn well like.

Sheila Hancock, Grumpy Old Women.

Have you ever noticed that anybody driving slower than you is an idiot, and anyone going faster than you is a maniac?

George Carlin

If I stop at a zebra crossing, I stop and wave and I'd like them to wave. But if they don't, then I think, 'Well, you bastard, this is the last time I'm gonna do this for you'.

Don Warrington, Grumpy Old Women.

Apparently more than 80 per cent of open-top sports cars are sold to sad sacks who believe this throbbing mechanical extension makes them look young and virile, not old and desperate.

Amanda Craig

I drive with my knees. Otherwise, how can I put on my lipstick and talk on my phone?

Sharon Stone

The worst drivers are women in people carriers, men in white vans and anyone in a baseball cap. That's just about everyone.

Paul O'Grady

You know, somebody actually complimented me on my driving today. They left a little note on the windscreen; it said 'Parking Fine.'

Tommy Cooper

As a senior citizen was driving down the freeway, his car phone rang. Answering, he heard his wife's voice urgently warning him, "Henry, I just heard on the news that there's a car going the wrong way on 280. Please be careful!" Henry said, "Hell, it's not just one car. It's hundreds of them!"

Anon

The best car safety device is a rear-view mirror with a cop in it.

Dudley Moore

Pounds, shillings and pence

Money isn't everything, but it sure keeps you in touch with your children.

J. Paul Getty

I've got all the money I'll ever need if I die by four o'clock this afternoon.

Henny Youngman

I'm living so far beyond my income that we may almost be said to be living apart.

e.e. cummings

There's no reason to be the richest man in the cemetery. You can't do any business from there.

Colonel Sanders

Another good thing about being poor is that when you are 70 your children will not have declared you legally insane in order to gain control of your estate.

Woody Allen

Vintage Vigour

I don't exercise. If God wanted me to bend over, he'd have put diamonds on the floor.

Joan Rivers

I get my exercise running to the funerals of my friends who exercise.

Barry Gray

I consider exercise vulgar. It makes people smell.

Alec Yuill Thornton

If God wanted me to touch my toes, he would have put them on my knees.

Roseanne Barr

I like long walks, especially when they are taken by people who annoy me.

Fred Allen

My idea of exercise is a good brisk sit down.

Phyllis Diller

Jogging is for people who aren't intelligent enough to watch television.

Victoria Wood

The trouble with jogging is that by the time you realize you're not in shape for it; it's too far to walk back.

Franklin P. Jones

I often take exercise. Only yesterday I had breakfast in bed.

Oscar Wilde

I bought all those celebrity exercise videos. I love to sit and eat cookies and watch them.

Dolly Parton

I have a punishing workout regimen. Every day I do three minutes on a treadmill, then I lie down, drink a glass of vodka and smoke a cigarette.

Anthony Hopkins

Sometimes I run around Regent's Park and go to the gym, I can manage about an hour, but stop for a cigarette every so often.

Julian Clary

A Quiet Five Minutes
THE AFTERNOON NAP

Sleep – those little slices of death, how I loathe them.

Edgar Allan Poe

No day is so bad it can't be fixed with a nap.

Carrie Snow

Two things I dislike about my granddaughter – when she won't take her afternoon nap, and when she won't let me take mine.

Gene Perret

Every businessman over 50 should have a daily nap and nip; a short nap after lunch and a relaxing highball before dinner.

Dr. Sara Murray Jordan

I have left orders to be awakened at any time in case of national emergency, even if I'm in a cabinet meeting.

Ronald Reagan

Menopausal Moments

YOU KNOW YOU'RE MENOPAUSAL WHEN...

...the dryer has shrunk every last pair of your jeans.

...everyone around you has an attitude problem.

...your husband is suddenly agreeing to everything you say.

...you're using your cellular phone to dial up every bumper sticker that says "How's my driving – call 1-800-***-."

...you're convinced there's a God and he's male.

...you can't believe they don't make a tampon bigger than Super Plus.

...you're sure that everyone is scheming to drive you crazy.

...the ibuprofen bottle is empty and you bought it yesterday.

All Anonymous

Male menopause is a lot more fun than female menopause. With female menopause you gain weight and get hot flashes. Male menopause – you get to date young girls and drive motorcycles.

Rita Rudner

I do get hot. Sometimes I think, "Oh I can smell the menopause on me." You know, it's kind of BO and Prozac and furniture polish.

Jenny Eclair, Grumpy Old Women.

For my sister's 50th birthday, I sent her a singing mammogram.

Steven Wright

I'm out of oestrogen and I've got a gun!

Bumper Sticker

The seven dwarves of menopause; itchy, bitchy, sweaty, sleepy, bloated, forgetful and psycho.

Anon

The Cracks of Time
FADING LOOKS

My face looks like a wedding cake left out in the rain.

W.H.Auden

As we get older, our bodies get shorter and our anecdotes get longer.

Robert Quillen

I guess I look like a rock quarry that someone has dynamited.

Charles Bronson

Like a lot of fellows around here, I have a furniture problem. My chest has fallen into my drawers.

Billy Casper

Many of my contemporaries have terrible feet, deformed by bunions, permanent corns and layers of dead skin like rock strata.

Sue Townsend

The problem with beauty is that it's like being born rich and getting poorer.

Joan Collins

I spent seven hours in a beauty shop – and that was just for the estimate.

Phyllis Diller

Take my photograph? You might as well use a picture of a relief map of Ireland!

Nancy Astor

I have a face like the behind of an elephant.

Charles Laughton

One day you look in the mirror and you realize that the face you are shaving is your father's.

Robert Harris

When I look in the mirror I don't see a rock star any more.
I see a little balding old guy who looks like someone's uncle.

Pete Townshend

Wrinkles should merely indicate where smiles have been.

Mark Twain

Folding Back the Years
COSMETIC SURGERY

I want to grow old without facelifts. I want to have the courage to be loyal to the face I have made.

Marilyn Monroe

I'd make plastic surgery compulsory for every woman over 40.

Simon Cowell

My husband said "show me your boobs" and I had to pull up my skirt… so it was time to get them done!

Dolly Parton

Look at Cher. One more face lift and she'll be wearing a beard.

Jennifer Saunders

Sylvester Stallone's mother's plastic surgery looks so bad it could have been bought through a mail order catalogue.

Graham Norton

If anybody says their facelift doesn't hurt, they're lying. It was like I'd spent the night with an axe murderer.

Sharon Osbourne

I was going to have cosmetic surgery until I noticed that the doctor's office was full of portraits by Picasso.

Rita Rudner

You know you're getting fat when you can pinch an inch on your forehead.

John Mendoza

In youth we run into difficulties. In old age difficulties run into us.

Beverly Sills

My Aching Bones!

HEALTH

First the doctor told me the good news: I was going to have a disease named after me.

Steve Martin

My father died of cancer when I was a teenager. He had it before it became popular.

Goodman Ace

You know you're getting old when everything hurts. And what doesn't hurt doesn't work.

Hy Gardner

I think it would be interesting if old people got anti-Alzheimer's disease where they slowly began to recover other people's lost memories.

George Carlin

The trouble with heart disease is that the first symptom is often hard to deal with – sudden death.

Michael Phelps

I am afraid… that health begins, after 70, and often long before, to have a meaning different from that which it had at 30. But it is culpable to murmur at the established order of the creation, as it is vain to oppose it. He that lives, must grow old; and he that would rather grow old than die, has God to thank for the infirmities of old age.

Samuel Johnson

I drive way too fast to worry about cholesterol.

Steven Wright

It's no longer a question of staying healthy. It's a question of finding a sickness you like.

Jackie Mason

I have finally come to the conclusion that a good reliable set of bowels is worth more to man than any quantity of brains.

Josh Billings

I'm not feeling very well, I need a doctor immediately. Ring the nearest golf course.

Groucho Marx

Doctor, Doctor
THE MEDICAL PROFESSION

The medics can now stretch life out for an additional dozen years but they don't tell you that most of these years are going to be spent flat on your back while some ghoul with thick glasses and a matted skull peers at you through a machine that's hot out of "Space Patrol".

Groucho Marx

Beware of the young doctor and the old barber.

Benjamin Franklin

Too many good docs are getting out of the business. Too many OB-GYNs aren't able to practise their love with women all across this country.

George W. Bush

The ultimate indignity is to be given a bedpan by a stranger who calls you by your first name.

Maggie Kuhn

Never go to a doctor whose office plants have died.

Erma Bombeck

My doctor gave me two weeks to live. I hope they are in August.

Ronnie Shakes

Our doctor would never really operate unless it was necessary. He was just that way. If he didn't need the money, he wouldn't lay a hand on you.

Herb Shriner

My doctor once said to me, "Do you think I'm here for the good of your health?"

Bob Monkhouse

A woman tells her doctor, "I've got a bad back." The doctor says, "It's old age." The woman says, "I want a second opinion." The doctor says: "Okay - you're ugly as well."

Tommy Cooper

My kid could get a bad X-ray and I could get a call from the doctor saying I have something growing in my bum and that would change my perspective on everything instantaneously, on what is and what is not important.

Tom Hanks

I've wrestled with reality for 35 years, and I'm happy, Doctor,
I finally won out over it.

Jimmy Stewart, Harvey

I kept thinking about that large, sweaty doctor who brought my
mother home after the first heart attack. He said, 'Don't ever get angry
at your mother, that might kill her.' That set off my demons, I think.

Gene Wilder

I told the doctor I broke my leg in two places. He told me to quit
going to those places.

Henny Youngman

Dad always thought laughter was the best medicine, which I guess
is why several of us died of tuberculosis.

Jack Handey

I don't know why people question the academic training of an
athlete. Fifty per cent of the doctors in this country graduated in
the bottom half of their classes.

Al McGuire

When I go in for a physical, they no longer ask how old I am.
They just carbon-date me.

Ronald Reagan

You Know You're Getting Old When...

…the only thing you want for your birthday is not to be reminded of it.

…"Happy Hour" turns out to be a nap!

…it takes you all night to do what you used to do all night

…you sink your teeth into an apple and they stay there!

…your back goes out more often than you do!

…you can't get your rocking chair started!

…it feels like the morning after and you haven't been anywhere.

…you get winded playing chess.

…being a little hippie does not have the same meaning as it did in the 60s.

…everything either dries up or leaks.

...you go for a mammogram and you realize it is the only time someone will ever ask you to appear topless in a film.

...your wife gives up sex for Lent, and you don't know till the 4th of July.

All Anonymous

...you've lost all your marvels.

Merry Browne

...you walk into a record store and everything you like has been marked down to $1.99.

Jack Simmons

...All the names in your black book have M.D. after them.

Arnold Palmer

...The candles cost more than the cake.

George Burns

The Good Old Days
MEMORIES

Nothing is more responsible for the good old days than a bad memory.

Franklin P. Adams

When I was young I was called a rugged individualist. When I was in my 50s I was considered eccentric. Here I am doing and saying the same things I did then and I'm labelled senile.

George Burns

We have all passed a lot of water since then.

Samuel Goldwyn

The one thing I remember about Christmas was that my father used to take me out in a boat about ten miles offshore on Christmas Day, and I used to have to swim back. Extraordinary. It was a ritual. Mind you, that wasn't the hard part. The difficult bit was getting out of the sack.

John Cleese

When I was a boy, the Dead Sea was only sick.

George Burns

When I was a kid my parents moved a lot, but I always found them.

Rodney Dangerfield

I was so naive as a kid I used to sneak behind the barn and do nothing.

Johnny Carson

Most people like the old days best – they were younger then.

Anon

I can remember when the air was clean and sex was dirty.

George Burns

There's a lot to do when you're a kid – spiders to catch, girls to poke in the eye – stuff to be getting on with.

Alan Davies

I remember when I was seven, sitting backstage in Vegas while these topless showgirls adjusted their G-strings in front of me. It was a strange way to grow up.

Donny Osmond

Nostalgia, the vice of the aged. We watch so many old movies our memories come in monochrome.

Angela Carter

The older a man gets, the farther he had to walk to school as a boy.

Anon

In every age "the good old days" were a myth. No one ever thought they were good at the time. For every age has consisted of crises that seemed intolerable to the people who lived through them.

Brooks Atkinson

Nostalgia is a file that removes the rough edges from the good old days.

Doug Larson

You don't appreciate a lot of stuff in school until you get older. Little things like being spanked every day by a middle-aged woman: stuff you pay good money for in later life.

Emo Philips

What's in An Age?

It is so comic to hear oneself called old, even at 90, I suppose!

Alice James

Age puzzles me. I thought it was a quiet time. My 70s were interesting and fairly serene, but my 80s are passionate. I grow more intense as I age.

Florida Scott-Maxwell

The hardest years in life are those between ten and 70.

Helen Hayes

People under 24 think old age starts around 55, those over 75, on the other hand, believe that youth doesn't end until the age of 58.

Alexander Chancellor

I'm 65 and I guess that puts me in with the geriatrics. But if there were 15 months in every year, I'd only be 48. That's the trouble with us. We number everything. Take women, for example. I think they deserve to have more than 12 years between the ages of 28 and 40.

James Thurber

No one is so old as to think he cannot live one more year.

Marcus T. Cicero

No woman should ever be quite accurate about her age. It looks so calculating.

Oscar Wilde

Who wants to be 95? 94-year-olds.

George Burns

The age of a woman doesn't mean a thing. The best tunes are played on the oldest fiddles.

Ralph Waldo Emerson

You can judge your age by the amount of pain you feel when you come in contact with a new idea.

John Nuveen

I do wish I could tell you my age but it's impossible. It keeps changing all the time.

Greer Garson

I am luminous with age.

Meridel Le Sueur

Age is not measured by years. Nature does not equally distribute energy. Some people are born old and tired while others are going strong at 70.

Dorothy Thompson

Your 50s are mature, reliable and dependable – or boring, predictable and conventional.

T. Kinnes

Old age is a special problem for me because I've never been able to shed the mental image I have of myself – a lad of about 19.

E.B. White

I'm 57. I can't look like a 30-year-old. You try to hold age at bay, but there comes a point when you just have to give up gracefully.

Elton John

You can calculate Zsa Zsa Gabor's age by the rings on her fingers.

Bob Hope

At 65 and drawing a state pension, I was delighted to discover that only people under 45 would regard me as old, even though sadly nobody would actually call me young.

Alexander Chancellor

Writing the Memoirs

I was born because it was a habit in those days, people didn't know anything else.

Will Rogers

My father had a profound influence on me, he was a lunatic.

Spike Milligan

I used to think I was an interesting person, but I must tell you how sobering a thought it is to realize your life's story fills about 35 pages and you have, actually, not much to say.

Roseanne Barr

I wanted to be president of the United States. I really did. The older I get, the less preposterous the idea seems.

Alec Baldwin

Thank goodness I was never sent to school: it would have rubbed off some of the originality.

Beatrix Potter

I succeeded by saying what everyone else is thinking.

Joan Rivers

I wrote the story myself. It's about a girl who lost her reputation and never missed it.

Mae West

When I was growing up, there were two things that were unpopular in my house. One was me, and the other was my guitar.

Bruce Springsteen

When I realized what I had turned out to be was a lousy, two-bit pool hustler and a drunk, I wasn't depressed at all. I was glad to have a profession.

Danny McGoorty, *Irish pool player.*

I always wanted to be an explorer, but – it seemed I was doomed to be nothing more than a very silly person.

Michael Palin

I have never described the time I was in *Doctor Who* as anything except a kind of ecstatic success, but all the rest has been rather a muddle and a disappointment. Compared to *Doctor Who*, it has been an outrageous failure really – it's so boring.

Tom Baker

An autobiography is an obituary in serial form with the last instalment missing.

Quentin Crisp

Rebecca was a busy liar in her distinguished old age, reinventing her past for gullible biographers.

Walter Clemons, on *Rebecca West.*

All I ever seemed to get was the kind of girl who had a special dispensation from Rome to wear the thickest part of her legs below the knee.

Hugh Leonard

I couldn't wait for success, so I went on ahead without it.

Jonathan Winters

I spent 90 per cent of my money on women and drink.
The rest I wasted.

George Best

On what?

Chris Eubank, *when asked if he had ever thought of writing an autobiography.*

I always knew looking back on my tears would bring me laughter, but I never knew looking back on my laughter would make me cry.

Cat Stevens

This bikini made me a success.

Ursula Andress

Forty pictures I was in, and all I remember is "What kind of bra will you be wearing today, honey?" That was always the area of big decision – from the neck to the navel.

Donna Reed

The really good idea is always traceable back quite a long way, often to a not very good idea which sparked off another idea that was only slightly better, which somebody else misunderstood in such a way that they then said something which was really rather interesting.

John Cleese

My toughest fight was with my first wife, and she won every round.

Muhammad Ali

I grew up in Europe, where the history comes from.

Eddie Izzard

It was no great tragedy being Judy Garland's daughter. I had tremendously interesting childhood years – except they had little to do with being a child.

Liza Minnelli

This is the second most bizarre thing ever to happen to me. The first was when I was sued by a woman who claimed she became pregnant because she watched me on TV and I bent her contraceptive coil.

Uri Geller

I wanted revenge; I wanted to dance on the graves of a few people who made me unhappy. It's a pretty infantile way to go through life – I'll show them – but I've done it, and I've got more than I ever dreamed of.

Anthony Hopkins

I sold the memoirs of my sex life to a publisher – they are going to make a board game out of it.

Woody Allen

Success didn't spoil me, I've always been insufferable.

Fran Lebowitz

I was coming home from kindergarten – well, they told me it was kindergarten. I found out later I had been working in a factory for ten years. It's good for a kid to know how to make gloves.

Ellen DeGeneres

My childhood was a period of waiting for the moment when I could send everyone and everything connected with it to hell.

Igor Stravinsky

I believe the true function of age is memory. I'm recording as fast as I can.

Rita Mae Brown

Nobody knows the age of the human race, but everybody agrees that it is old enough to know better.

Anon

I come from a family where gravy is considered a beverage.

Erma Bombeck

The Trouble Today is...

We live in an age when pizza gets to your home before the police.
Jeff Marder

It's easy to identify people who can't count to ten. They're in front of you in the supermarket express lane.
M. Grundler

Too bad that all the people who know how to run the country are driving taxi cabs and cutting hair.
George Burns

The trouble with being punctual is that nobody's there to appreciate it.
Franklin P. Jones

The rage that happens in shops happens, normally, because of bad service. There's appalling service in Britain. Appalling. I mean unimaginably dire service, and we all put up with it.
India Knight, Grumpy Old Women.

The youth of the present day are quite monstrous. They have absolutely no respect for dyed hair.
Oscar Wilde

I am amazed at radio DJs today. I am firmly convinced that AM on my radio stands for Absolute Moron. I will not begin to tell you what FM stands for.

Jasper Carrott

We've all seen them, on the street corners, many of them smoking, many of them on drugs; they've got no jobs to go to, and once a week we see them queuing for the state hand-outs – or pensions, as we call them.

Harry Hill

What about safety matches? I never get that. What is a safety match? What does that mean? It's a box of matches you could ignite; you could burn a house down.

Nigel Havers, Grumpy Old Men.

Newspapers are unable, seemingly, to discriminate between a bicycle accident and the collapse of civilisation.

George Bernard Shaw

You can say this for ready-mixes – the next generation isn't going to have any trouble making pies exactly like mother used to make.

Earl Wilson

We are living in a world today where lemonade is made from artificial flavours and furniture polish is made from real lemons.

Alfred E. Newman

You can find your way across this country using burger joints the way a navigator uses stars.

Charles Kuralt

Few cultures have not produced the idea that in some past era the world ran better than it does now.

Elizabeth Janeway

Now there are more overweight people in America than average-weight people. So overweight people are now average. Which means you've met your New Year's resolution.

Jay Leno

Pol Pot killed 1.7 million Cambodians, died under house arrest, well done there. Stalin killed many millions, died in his bed, aged 72, well done indeed. And the reason we let them get away with it is they killed their own people. And we're sort of fine with that.

Hitler killed people next door. Oh, stupid man. After a couple of years we won't stand for that, will we?

Eddie Izzard

What some people mistake for the high cost of living is really the cost of high living.

Doug Larson

Nowadays men lead lives of noisy desperation.

James Thurber

If God had wanted us to vote, he would have given us candidates.

Jay Leno

The trouble with political jokes is that very often they get elected.

Will Rogers

My husband gave me a necklace. It's fake. I requested fake. Maybe I'm paranoid, but in this day and age, I don't want something around my neck that's worth more than my head.

Rita Rudner

If life were fair, Dan Quayle would be making a living asking, "Do you want fries with that?"

John Cleese

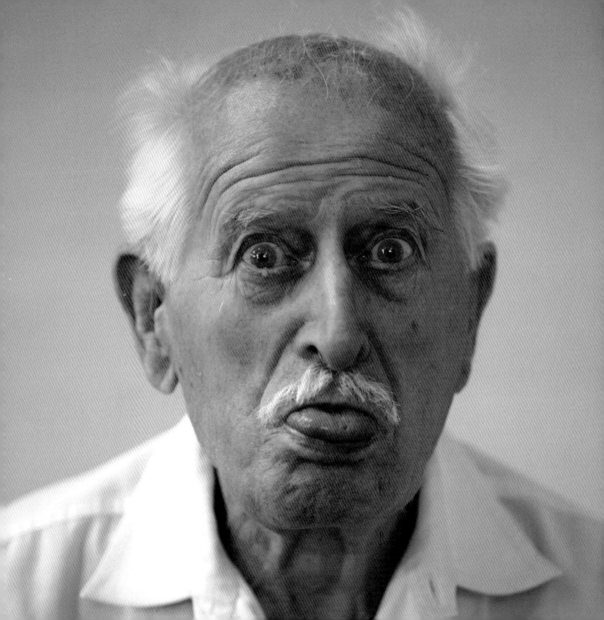

I Don't Believe it!

GROANS AND GRIPES

There are three intolerable things in life – cold coffee, lukewarm champagne and overexcited women.

Orson Welles

My 50 years have shown me that few people know what they are talking about. I don't mean idiots that don't know. I mean everyone.

John Cleese

Every year, back comes Spring, with nasty little birds yapping their fool heads off and the ground all mucked up with plants.

Dorothy Parker

The vote means nothing to women. We should be armed.

Edna O'Brien

Midlife can bring out your angry, bitter side. You look at your latte-swilling, beeper-wearing know-it all teenager and think, "For this I have stretch marks?"

Anon

The countryside is incredibly boring. There's lots of shagging, lots of murders, lots of sarcasm, lots of treachery, and lots of bad cooking, but it's all hidden. You've got all the space and the flowers, but it's dull!

Tom Baker

There is a remarkable breakdown of taste and intelligence at Christmas time. Mature, responsible grown men wear neckties made of holly leaves and drink alcoholic beverages with raw egg yolks in them.

P.J. O'Rourke

I tell you what really turns my toes up: love scenes with 68-year-old men and actresses young enough to be their granddaughter.

Mel Gibson

Potpourri. I even find the name irritating. Potpourri.

John O'Farrell, Grumpy Old Men.

If I were reincarnated, I would wish to be returned to Earth as a killer virus to lower human population levels.

Prince Philip

I have always hated that damn James Bond. I'd like to kill him.

Sean Connery

Few things are more satisfying than seeing your own children have teenagers of their own.

Doug Larson

I am so busy doing nothing… that the idea of doing anything – which as you know, always leads to something – cuts into the nothing and then forces me to have to drop everything.

Jerry Seinfeld

A healthy male adult bore consumes each year one and a half times his own weight in other people's patience.

John Updike

I'm convinced there's a small room in the attic of the Foreign Office where future diplomats are taught to stammer.

Peter Ustinov

A lot of people like snow. I find it to be an unnecessary freezing of water.

Carl Reiner

An intellectual snob is someone who can listen to the William Tell Overture and not think of *The Lone Ranger.*

Dan Rather

Life is a Cruise

I love flying. I've been to almost as many places as my luggage.

Bob Hope

The great and recurring question about abroad is, is it worth getting there?

Rose Macaulay

Abroad is unutterably bloody and foreigners are fiends.

Nancy Mitford

The scientific theory I like best is that the rings of Saturn are composed entirely of lost airline luggage.

Mark Russell

I don't hold with abroad and think foreigners speak English when our backs are turned.

Quentin Crisp

I wouldn't mind seeing China if I could come back the same day.

Philip Larkin

Grandparents Know Best

If I had known my grandchildren would be so much fun I would have had them first!

Anon

My grandmother took a bath every year, whether she needed it or not.

Brendan Behan

Grandchildren are God's way of compensating us for growing old.

Mary H. Waldrip

An hour with your grandchildren can make you feel young again. Anything longer than that, and you start to age quickly.

Gene Perret

The best babysitters, of course, are the baby's grandparents. You feel completely comfortable entrusting your baby to them for long periods, which is why most grandparents flee to Florida.

Dave Barry

Technophobes and Technophiles

How can I believe in God when just last week I got my tongue caught in the roller of an electric typewriter?

Woody Allen

I am not the only person who uses his computer mainly for the purpose of diddling with his computer.

Dave Barry

It is only when they go wrong that machines remind you how powerful they are.

Clive James

The thing with high-tech is that you always end up using scissors.

David Hockney

I get in a complete rage with the computer. I get all hot, my hair is standing on end, I look like a clown trying to control myself… Then I get up and walk away and the bloody egg-timer on the screen is still there.

Nina Myskow, Grumpy Old Women.

I hate television. I hate it as much as peanuts. But I can't stop eating peanuts.

Orson Welles

Her own mother lived the latter years of her life in the horrible suspicion that electricity was dripping invisibly all over the house.

James Thurber

Buying the right computer and getting it to work properly is no more complicated than building a nuclear reactor from wristwatch parts in a darkened room using only your teeth.

Dave Barry

A new Viagra virus is going round the Internet. It doesn't affect your hard drive, but you can't minimize anything for hours.

Joan Rivers

Every time you think television has hit its lowest ebb, a new programme comes along to make you wonder where you thought the ebb was.

Art Buchwald

I don't want to retire. I'm not that good at crossword puzzles.

Norman Mailer

Life is...

...like a sewer. What you get out of it depends on what you put into it.

Tom Lehrer

...like a play: it's not the length, but the excellence of the acting that matters.

Seneca

...the art of drawing without an eraser.

Anon

...the art of drawing sufficient conclusions from insufficient data.

Samuel Butler

...a sexually transmitted disease and the mortality rate is 100 per cent.

R.D. Laing

...hard. After all, it kills you.

Katharine Hepburn

...a tragedy when seen in close-up, but a comedy in long-shot.

Charlie Chaplin

Famous Last Words

On the contrary.

Henrik Ibsen, *after hearing a nurse remark that he was feeling better.*

Bugger Bognor.

George V, *having been assured by his physician that he would soon be fit enough to holiday in Bognor Regis.*

I've had 18 straight whiskies, I think that's the record...

Dylan Thomas

My wallpaper and I are fighting a duel to the death. One or the other of us has to go.

Oscar Wilde

This isn't *Hamlet*, you know, it's not meant to go into the bloody ear.

Laurence Olivier, *to his nurse, who had spilt water on him.*

If this is dying, I don't think much of it.

Lytton Strachey

Index

Picture Credits

The publishers would like to thank the following sources for their kind permission to reproduce the pictures in this book:

© iStockphoto.com: 22, 33, 48, 51, 58–59, 62–63, 70, 74, 94, 108, 116, 143; /Chad Anderson: 6–7; /Grigory Bibikov: 28–29; /Nilgun Bostanci: 146; /Patrick Breig: 19; /Joan Vicent Canto Roig: 14; /Luca di Filippo: 25; /Diane Diederich: 66; /Sharon Dominick: 97; /Micheline Dube: 90; /Jami Garrison: 154–155; /Scott Griessel: 82–83; /Stephan Hoerold: 112; /Steve Luker: 10, 129; /Carmen Martinez Banus: 54; /Oleg Prikhodko: 132; /Vinicius Ramalho Tupinamba: 44; /Pali Rao: 120; /Joerg Reimann: 78; /Jacom Stephens: 36; /Dan Talson: 41; /Bela Tibor Kozma: 136; /Annett Vauteck: 104–105; /Duncan Walker: 150; /Serdar Yagci: 100; /Lisa F Young: 86–87, 125